Design: Jill Coote
Recipe Photography: Peter Barry
Jacket and Illustration Artwork: Jane Winton,
courtesy of Bernard Thornton Artists, London
Editors: Jillian Stewart, Kate Cranshaw and Laura Potts

CLB 3514
Published by Grange Books,
an imprint of Grange Books PLC,
The Grange, Grange Yard, London.
© 1994 CLB Publishing,
Godalming, Surrey, England.
All rights reserved.
Printed and bound in Singapore
Published 1994
ISBN 1-85627-419-5

THE LITTLE BOOK ·OF·

Barbecues

*A selection of innovative barbecue recipes
to help you to make the most of summer
cookery.*

Grange BOOKS

Introduction

$\mathcal{T}$he glorious days and warm evenings of summer signal the chance to enjoy some long lunches and suppers eaten out of doors. Eating *al fresco* is both relaxed and informal and, though temperamental weather means that the tradition is not as developed in Britain as it is in southern Europe, it is a style of eating that continues to grow in popularity. Certainly it is hard to beat the taste of food cooked over an open grill and the distinctive smell of barbecued food is one of the most evocative of summer.

There are two basic categories into which barbecues can be divided. At its most basic a barbecue need only be an old grill resting on some bricks over a heat source. Home-made, open barbecues like these are cheap and effective, though it can be difficult to control temperature on them. More sophisticated open barbecues can be bought commercially and range in size from the small hibachi type to the larger trolley barbecues. Covered barbecues, such as kettle barbecues and gas grills, make up the second category. They convect heat and cook in much the same way as a traditional oven rather than through direct heat as in an open, grill barbecue. Though traditionalists may have reservations about them, they are easier to use, making temperature and cooking time easier to gauge.

There are several types of fuel that can be used for barbecuing, each of which has its advocates. For big grill barbecues wood can be used, though it is important to ensure that it is really dry before you begin. To get the very best results when using wood as your fuel, do not start cooking until the flames have died down and the wood has become embers. This ensures that the food does not get scorched. Charcoal and barbecue briquets are the most commonly used form of barbecue fuel. They have the advantage over wood in that you can accurately judge just how much you are going to need to be able to cook your food. By combining charcoal with barbecue briquets it is possible to avoid the problem of fuel not lasting long enough to cook large pieces of meat – a problem that is common when using solely charcoal.

Though a good barbecue and reliable fuel are important to the success of a barbecued meal, careful preparation of the food is also vital. Food is cooked at a very high temperature on a barbecue and must be properly marinated to ensure that it does not become tough or dried out in the cooking process. Marinades vary, though many are oil and wine based, with garlic, herbs and spices added to give flavour.

This book provides a selection of delicious recipes that give new ideas on how to prepare meat, fish and vegetables to barbecue, giving you the chance to experiment with new and delicious combinations of flavours rather than relying on tried and tested favourites.

Monkfish and Pepper Kebabs with Bearnaise Butter Sauce

SERVES 4

Monkfish is a firm, succulent white fish, ideal for kebabs.

PREPARATION: 30 mins
COOKING: 15-20 mins

---

8 rashers streaky bacon, bone and rind
    removed
2 pieces lemon grass
900g/2lbs monkfish, cut into 5cm/2-inch pieces
1 green and red pepper, cut into 5cm/2-inch
    pieces
12 button mushrooms, washed and trimmed
8 bay leaves
Oil for brushing
120ml/4 fl oz dry white wine
60ml/4 tbsps tarragon vinegar
2 shallots, finely chopped
1 tbsp chopped fresh chervil or parsley
225g/8oz butter, melted
Salt and pepper

---

1. Cut the bacon in half lengthways and then
in half across. Peel the lemon grass and use
only the soft core. Cut this into small shreds.

2. Place a piece of fish on each piece of bacon
and top with a shred of lemon grass. Roll up the
bacon around the fish. Thread each roll onto

Step 2 Place a piece of fish onto a strip of bacon and top with a shred of lemon grass. Roll and thread onto kebab skewers.

kebab skewers, alternating with the peppers,
mushrooms and bay leaves. Brush well with
oil.

3. Cook on an oiled rack over hot coals for
15-20 minutes, turning frequently and brushing
with more oil, if necessary, until the fish is
cooked.

4. Heat together the wine, vinegar and shallots
in a small saucepan until they are boiling. Cook
rapidly until reduced by half.

5. Stir in the herbs and lower the heat. Beat in
the butter, a little at a time, until the sauce is the
thickness of an hollandaise. Season to taste and
serve with the kebabs.

Turkey and Pancetta Rolls

SERVES 4-6

Serve these stylish rolled turkey escalopes with a mixed leaf salad and rice.

PREPARATION: 30 mins
COOKING: 20-30 mins

---

2 turkey breasts, 460g/1lb each, skinned
90g/3oz butter softened
1 clove garlic, crushed
1 tbsp oregano leaves
Salt and pepper
16 slices pancetta or prosciutto ham
Oil

---

1. Cut the turkey breasts in half, lengthwise. Place each piece between two sheets of dampened greaseproof paper and bat out with a rolling pin or meat mallet to flatten.

2. Mix the butter, garlic, oregano and salt and pepper together.

3. Spread half of the mixture over each slice of turkey. Lay 4 slices of pancetta on top of each piece of turkey.

4. Roll each turkey escalope up, tucking in the sides and tie with fine string in 3 places. Spread the remaining garlic butter on the outside of each roll.

5. Cook the rolls over medium hot coals for 20-30 minutes, or until tender. A meat thermometer inserted into the centre of each roll should read 90°C/190°F.

6. Slice each roll into 1.25cm/½-inch rounds to serve.

Scallop, Bacon and Prawn Kebabs

SERVES 4

Don't overcook these kebabs or the scallops will become tough.

PREPARATION: 25 mins
COOKING: 15-20 mins

---

12 large, raw scallops
12 rashers smoked streaky bacon
12 raw king prawns peeled and de-veined
Juice of 1 lemon
2 tbsps oil
Coarsely ground black pepper

Red chilli yogurt sauce
3 slices bread, crusts removed, soaked in water
2 cloves garlic, finely chopped
1 red chilli, chopped
1 large canned red pimento
3 tbsps olive oil
140ml/¼ pint natural yogurt

---

1. Wrap each scallop in a rasher of bacon and thread onto skewers, alternating with the prawns.

2. Mix the lemon juice, oil and pepper and brush over the shellfish. Cook on a wire rack over medium hot coals for 15-20 minutes. Turn frequently and cook until the bacon is lightly crisped and the scallops are just firm.

3. Meanwhile, prepare the sauce. Squeeze the bread to remove the water and place the bread in a blender.

4. Add the garlic, chilli and pimento and blend well.

5. With the machine running, pour in the oil through the funnel in a thin, steady stream.

6. Keep the machine running until the mixture is a smooth, shiny paste.

7. Combine with the yogurt and mix well. Serve with the kebabs.

Barbecued Steak

Cooking one large steak means that everyone gets fed at once!

PREPARATION: 25 mins
COOKING: 30-45 mins

1.5kg/3½lb skirt steak

Barbecue seasoning
1½ tbsps salt
½ tsp freshly ground pepper
½ tsp cayenne pepper (or paprika for a milder tasting mixture)

Barbecue sauce
60ml/4 tbsps oil
340ml/12 fl oz passata
3 tbsps Worcestershire sauce
90ml/6 tbsps cider vinegar
60g/4 tbsps soft brown sugar
60ml/4 tbsps chopped onion
1 clove garlic, crushed
1 bay leaf
60ml/4 tbsps water
2 tsps dry mustard
Dash Tabasco
Salt and pepper

1. First prepare the barbecue sauce. Combine all the ingredients, reserving salt and pepper to add later.

2. Cook the sauce in a heavy pan over a low heat for 30 minutes, stirring frequently and adding more water if the sauce reduces too quickly.

3. Remove the bay leaf and add salt and pepper to taste before using. The sauce should be thick.

4. Score the meat across both sides with a large knife. Mix together the barbecue seasoning and rub all over the meat.

5. Sear the meat on both sides on an oiled grill rack just above the hot coals. Raise the rack, baste the meat with the barbecue sauce and grill slowly for 30-45 minutes, depending on taste.

6. During last 5 minutes, lower the rack and grill the meat quickly on both sides, still basting with the sauce.

7. Slice the meat thinly across the grain and serve with any remaining sauce.

Lamb Kebabs

SERVES 4

Meat kebabs are a typical Greek dish and these have all the characteristic flavours –
oregano, garlic, lemon and olive oil.

PREPARATION: 20 mins, plus marinating
COOKING: 10-20 mins

680g/1½lbs lean lamb from the leg or neck fillet
Juice of 1 large lemon
90ml/6 tbsps olive oil
1 clove garlic, crushed
1 tbsp chopped fresh oregano
1 tbsp chopped fresh thyme
Salt and pepper
2 medium onions
Fresh bay leaves

---

1. Trim the meat of excess fat and cut it into
5cm/2-inch cubes. Mix together the remaining

Step 1 Cut the meat into even-sized cubes.

Step 3 Thread the meat and bay leaves onto skewers and slip the onion rings over the meat.

ingredients except the bay leaves and the
onions. Pour the mixture into a shallow dish.

2. Add the meat to the marinade and turn to
coat completely. Cover and leave to marinate
for at least four hours, or overnight.

3. To assemble the kebabs, remove the meat
from the marinade and thread onto skewers,
alternating with the fresh bay leaves.

4. Slice the onions into rings and slip the rings
over the meat on the skewers.

5. Place the kebabs on the oiled grill rack over
hot coals, and grill for about 5-10 minutes per
side basting frequently. Pour over any
remaining marinade to serve.

Marsala Fish

SERVES 4

Barbecued whole fish make a delicious alternative to burgers and kebabs.

PREPARATION: 25 mins
COOKING: 10-15 mins

---

4 medium mackerel, trout or similar whole fish,
    cleaned
2 tsps turmeric
Pinch ground cinnamon
Pinch ground cloves
1 small piece ginger, grated
Juice of 1 lemon
60ml/4 tbsps oil
2 green chillies, finely chopped
1 clove garlic, crushed
Salt and pepper
Fresh coriander leaves

Accompaniment
½ cucumber, finely diced

140ml/¼ pint thick set natural yogurt
1 spring onion, finely chopped
Salt and pepper

---

1. Cut three slits into each side of the fish.
Combine the spices, lemon juice, oil, garlic,
chillies and salt and pepper, and spread over
the fish and inside the cuts.

2. Place whole sprigs of coriander inside the
fish. Brush the grill rack lightly with oil or use a
wire fish rack.

3. Cook the fish for 10-15 minutes, turning
often and basting with any remaining mixture.

4. Combine the accompaniment ingredients
and serve with the fish.

Zanzibar Prawns

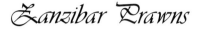

SERVES 4
King prawns make impressive kebabs.

PREPARATION: 25 mins
COOKING: 18-23 mins

460g/1lb king prawns, peeled and de-veined
1 large fresh pineapple, peeled, cored and cut
  into chunks
Oil

Sauce
Remaining pineapple
140ml/¼ pint orange juice
1 tbsp vinegar
1 tbsp lime juice
1 tsp dry mustard
1 tbsp brown sugar

1. Alternately thread the prawns and pineapple pieces onto skewers, using about 4 pineapple pieces per skewer.

2. Place the remaining pineapple and the rest of the sauce ingredients into a food processor and purée.

3. Pour into a small pan and cook over low heat for about 10-15 minutes to reduce slightly.

4. Place the kebabs on a lightly oiled rack above medium hot coals and cook about 6 minutes, turning and basting frequently with the sauce.

5. Sprinkle the cooked kebabs with a little flaked coconut and serve on chicory leaves. Serve the remaining sauce separately.

Seekh Kababs

MAKES 18

These spicy Indian kebabs are delicious.

PREPARATION: 15-20 mins
COOKING: 12-16 mins

Juice of ½ lemon
2 tbsps chopped fresh mint
3-4 tbsps chopped coriander leaves
30g/1oz raw cashew nuts
1 medium onion, coarsley chopped
2 cloves garlic, chopped
1-2 fresh green chillies, seeded and finely
    chopped
680g/1½lb lean mince, beef or lamb
2 tsps ground coriander
2 tsps ground cumin
1 tsp ground caraway seeds
½ tsp garam masala
½ tsp Tandoori colour
1 egg yolk
¼ tsp chilli powder
Salt and pepper

*Grind the following ingredients in a coffee
    grinder:*

2 tbsps white poppy seeds
2 tbsps sesame seeds

---

1. Put the first seven ingredients into a liquidiser and blend to a smooth paste. Transfer the mixture to a large bowl.

2. Using the liquidiser, grind the mince in 2-3 batches until it is fairly smooth; add to the liquidised ingredients in the bowl.

3. Add the rest of the ingredients and process in a food processor, until the mixture is smooth.

4. Chill for 30 minutes.

5. Divide the mix into 18 balls.

6. Mould each ball onto a skewer and form into a sausage shape about 10-13cm/4-5 inches long.

7. Brush generously with oil and place on an oiled rack just above coals. Cook for 6-8 minutes, brush with more oil and cook for a further 6-8 minutes.

Mustard Grilled Pork with Poppy Seeds

SERVES 4-6

To serve the pork, slice thinly and accompany with the remaining sauce.

PREPARATION: 20 mins, plus marinating
COOKING: 45 mins-1 hr

4 × 175-200g/6-7oz whole pork fillets/
   tenderloin
2 tbsps black poppy seeds

Marinade
1 tbsp mild mustard
60ml/4 tbsps oil
60ml/4 tbsps unsweetened apple juice
1 clove garlic, crushed
Salt and pepper

Sweet mustard sauce
280ml/½ pint mild mustard
60g/2oz demerara sugar
60ml/2 fl oz dry cider
2 tsps chopped fresh tarragon
Pinch cayenne pepper

Salt

1. Mix the marinade ingredients together and rub into the pork. Place in a dish, cover and refrigerate for 4 hours or overnight.

2. Using a barbecue with an adjustable grill rack, place the pork over the coals on the highest level. Cook for 45 minutes-1 hour, basting with the marinade and turning frequently.

3. Lower the shelf and baste frequently with the sauce during the last 10 minutes of cooking time.

4. During the last 5 minutes, sprinkle the pork fillets with the poppy seeds.

5. Combine the sauce ingredients, adding salt to taste. Serve with the grilled pork.

Boti Kabab

SERVES 6

Tender boneless lamb is the traditional meat used for these Indian kababs.

PREPARATION: 20 mins, plus marinating
COOKING: 16-22 mins

680g/1½lbs boned leg of lamb
2 cloves garlic, chopped
2 tbsps chopped coriander leaves
2 tbsps lemon juice
90g/3oz thick-set natural yogurt
Salt to taste
½ tsp ground turmeric

Grind the following 4 ingredients in a coffee grinder:

6 green cardamom pods
2.5cm/1-inch cinnamon stick
2-3 dried red chillies
1 tbsp coriander seeds

---

1. Prick the meat all over with a sharp knife

and cut into 4cm/1½-inch cubes.

2. Put the garlic, coriander leaves, lemon juice and yogurt into a liquidiser or food processor and blend until smooth. Add all the remaining ingredients.

3. Put the meat into a bowl and add the liquidised ingredients. Mix thoroughly, cover and leave to marinate for 6-8 hours.

4. Thread the meat onto skewers leaving about a 5mm/¼-inch gap between each piece. Mix any remaining marinade with 2 tbsps oil and keep aside.

5. Place the skewers on an oiled grill rack over medium hot coals for 2-3 minutes on each side. Adjust the rack to the top position. Brush the kababs with the marinade mixture and grill for 6-8 minutes. Repeat for the other side.

Indian Chicken

SERVES 4-6

Spiced yogurt makes a delicious coating for chicken pieces.

PREPARATION: 15 mins, plus marinating
COOKING: 45-55 mins

---

1 × 1.4kg/3lb chicken, cut into 8 joints
570ml/1 pint natural yogurt
2 tsps ground coriander
2 tsps paprika
1 tsp ground turmeric
Juice of 1 lime
1 tbsp honey
½ clove garlic, crushed
1 small piece fresh ginger, peeled and grated

---

1. Pierce the chicken all over with a fork or skewer. Combine all the remaining ingredients and spread half the mixture over the chicken, rubbing in well.

2. Place the chicken in a shallow dish or a plastic bag and cover or tie and leave for at least 4 hours or overnight in the refrigerator.

3. Using a barbecue with an adjustable rack, arrange the chicken skin side down and grill on the level furthest from the coals. Grill for 15-20 minutes or until lightly browned, turn over and cook again until lightly browned. Baste frequently with the remaining marinade.

4. Lower the grill for the last 15 minutes and cook, turning and basting frequently, until the chicken is brown and the skin is crisp.

5. Serve any remaining yogurt mixture separately as a sauce.

Sausage, Apple & Pepper Kebabs

SERVES 6

Perfect for summer barbecues, these kebabs are unusual, easy and inexpensive.

PREPARATION: 15 mins plus marinating
COOKING: 5-6 mins

140ml/¼ pint honey (set)
1 tsp chopped fresh dill
120ml/4 fl oz white wine vinegar
460g/1lb ham sausage, cut in 5cm/2 inch
   pieces
2 large cooking apples
1 large red pepper

---

1. Mix together the honey and dill. Gradually whisk in the vinegar to blend thoroughly. Add the sausage, stirring to coat evenly and allow to marinate for about 2 hours.

Step 1 Mix the honey and herbs together and gradually beat in the vinegar.

Step 3 Cut peppers in half and remove the core and seeds. Also cut out any white pith as this tends to be bitter.

2. Cut the apples in quarters and remove the cores. Cut in half again crossways or lengthways.

3. Cut the pepper in half. Chop into pieces about the same size as the sausage and apple.

4. Thread the ingredients onto skewers, alternating the pepper, sausage and apple.

5. Brush with the marinade and place over hot coals on an oiled grill rack. Cook for about 5-6 minutes, turning 2 or 3 times and brushing frequently with the marinade. Pour over any additional marinade to serve.

Pork Burgers

SERVES 4

This recipe uses lean minced pork, and so makes for a healthier burger.

PREPARATION: 20 mins
COOKING: 15 mins

460g/1lb extra lean, raw minced pork
1 small onion, finely chopped
60g/2oz fresh wholemeal breadcrumbs
1 stock cube, crumbled
1 tsp chopped fresh parsley
Salt and black pepper, to taste
1 tbsp tomato purée
1 tsp made mustard
1 egg, beaten

To serve
4 wholemeal baps
Crisp lettuce leaves and tomato and cucumber
 slices

1. In a large bowl, mix together the minced pork, onion and breadcrumbs.

Step 2 Add the remaining burger ingredients to the mince and onion mixture. Mix them together thoroughly.

2. Stir in all the remaining burger ingredients and mix together thoroughly. Divide into quarters, and form each into a hamburger shape with lightly floured hands.

3. Arrange the burgers on an oiled grill rack and cook over hot coals for 7-8 minutes on each side, turning the burgers to prevent them burning.

4. Serve in wholemeal baps with lettuce, sliced tomato and cucumber.

Turkey Kebabs

SERVES 6

For ease use the ready-prepared turkey joints which are now easily available from supermarkets or butchers.

PREPARATION: 20 mins, plus marinating
COOKING: 20-30 mins

1.4kg/3lbs lean turkey meat
2 tsps fresh chopped sage
1 sprig rosemary, chopped
Juice 1 lemon
2 tbsps olive oil
Salt and freshly ground black pepper
120g/4oz lean back bacon, rind removed
Whole sage leaves

1. Remove any bone from the turkey and cut the meat into even-sized cubes.

2. Put the chopped sage, rosemary, lemon

Step 3 Cut the bacon in half lengthways and again crosswise.

Step 4
Carefully roll the marinated turkey in the strips of bacon.

juice, oil, salt and pepper into a large bowl and stir in the turkey meat, mixing well to coat evenly. Cover and refrigerate overnight.

3. Cut the bacon rashers in half lengthways and then crosswise.

4. Wrap these pieces around as many of the cubes of marinated turkey meat as possible.

5. Thread the turkey and bacon rolls alternately with the whole sage leaves and any unwrapped turkey cubes onto kebab skewers.

6. Cook the kebabs over medium hot coals for '20-30 minutes, turning frequently and basting with the marinade whilst cooking. Serve immediately.

35

Niçoise Chicken

SERVES 4

In this recipe, a raw tomato sauce makes the perfect accompaniment to olive-stuffed chicken.

PREPARATION: 30 mins, plus chilling
COOKING: 20-25 mins

4 boned chicken breasts, unskinned
60ml/4 tbsps oil
2 tbsps lemon juice

Filling
460g/1lb large black olives, pitted
2 tbsps capers
1 clove garlic, roughly chopped
4 canned anchovy fillets
2 tbsps olive oil

Sauce
460g/1lb ripe tomatoes, skinned, seeded and
    chopped
1 shallot, very finely chopped
2 tbsps chopped parsley
2 tbsps chopped basil
2 tbsps white wine vinegar
2 tbsps olive oil
1 tbsp sugar

Salt and pepper
1 tbsp tomato purée

1. Cut a pocket into the thickest side of each of the chicken breasts.

2. Combine half the olives, half the capers and the remaining ingredients for the filling in a blender or food processor.

3. Work to a purée. Add the remaining olives and capers and process a few times to chop them roughly.

4. Fill the chicken breasts with the mixture and chill to help firm.

5. Baste the skin side of the chicken with the oil and lemon juice mixed together. Cook skin side down first for 10-15 minutes over medium hot coals.

6. Turn over, baste again and grill for another 10 minutes on the other side.

7. Meanwhile, combine the sauce ingredients and mix together very well. Serve with the chicken.

Swordfish Kebabs

Swordfish is a firm-fleshed fish, so it won't fall apart during cooking.

PREPARATION: 15 mins
COOKING: 10 mins

1kg/2¼lbs swordfish steaks
90ml/6 tbsps olive oil
1 tsp chopped oregano
1 tsp chopped marjoram
Juice and rind of ½ lemon
4 tomatoes, cut in thick slices
2 lemons, cut in thin slices
Salt and freshly ground pepper
Lemon slices and parsley, for garnish

Step 1 Cut the swordfish steaks into even-sized pieces.

Step 3 Thread the ingredients onto the skewers, alternating the colours.

1. Cut the swordfish steaks into 5cm/2-inch pieces.

2. Mix the olive oil, herbs, lemon juice and rind together and set it aside.

3. Thread the swordfish, tomato slices and lemon slices onto skewers, alternating the ingredients.

4. Brush the skewers with the oil and lemon juice mixture and cook on an oiled grill rack over hot coals for about 10 minutes, basting frequently with the lemon and oil.

5. Serve garnished with lemon slices and parsley.

Butterflied Lamb

SERVES 6-8

To make preparation easy, get a butcher to 'butterfly' the lamb for you.

PREPARATION: 40 mins, plus marinating
COOKING: 40-50 mins

1.8kg/4lb leg of lamb
75ml/5 tbsps oil
Juice and rind of one lemon
Small bunch mint, roughly chopped
Salt and coarsely ground black pepper
1 clove garlic, crushed

---

1. To butterfly the lamb, cut through the skin along the line of the main bone down to the bone.

2. Cut the meat away from the bone, opening out the leg while scraping against the bone with a small, sharp knife. Take out the bone and remove the excess fat.

3. Flatten thick parts by batting with a rolling pin or meat mallet.

4. Alternatively, make shallow cuts halfway through the thickest parts and press open.

5. Thread two or three long skewers through the meat – this will make the meat easier to handle and turn on the grill.

6. Place in a large, shallow dish. Mix the other ingredients together and pour over the lamb, rubbing it in well.

7. Cover the dish and refrigerate overnight. Turn the lamb frequently.

8. Remove the lamb from the dish and reserve the marinade.

9. Grill at least 15cm/6 inches away from the coals on the skin side first. Grill for 20 minutes per side for pink lamb and 30-40 minutes per side for more well done meat.

10. Baste frequently during grilling. Remove the skewers and cut the slices across the grain to serve.

11. Alternatively, roast the lamb in a 180°C/350°F/Gas Mark 4 oven for half of the cooking time and grill on the barbecue for the last half of cooking.

Mexican Kebabs

SERVES 4

The spice mixture and sauce give these their Mexican flavour, serve with rice and taco sauce.

PREPARATION: 15 mins, plus marinating
COOKING: 15-20 mins

460g/1lb pork or lamb, cut into 5cm/2 inch
   pieces
120g/4oz large button mushrooms, left whole
2 medium onions, quartered
8 bay leaves
1 tsp cocoa powder
2 tsps chilli powder
¼ tsp garlic powder
½ tsp dried marjoram
Salt and pepper
90ml/6 tbsps oil

1. Put meat and mushrooms in a bowl, add the remaining ingredients and stir to coat well.

2. Cover the bowl and leave to marinate at least 6 hours, preferably overnight.

3. Remove the meat, mushrooms and bay leaves from the marinade and reserve it. Thread onto skewers, alternating meat, onions, mushrooms and bay leaves.

Step 1 Place meat and mushrooms in a deep bowl with the marinade ingredients and stir to coat thoroughly.

4. Place on an oiled grill rack over hot coals for 15-20 minutes, turning and basting frequently. The lamb may be served pink.

Step 3 Thread the meat and mushrooms onto skewers, alternating with onions and bay leaves.

Index